A Sky That We Might Reach

Yonas Campbell

BookLeaf
Publishing

India | USA | UK

Presentation by *BookLeaf Publishing*

Web: www.bookleafpub.com

E-mail: info@bookleafpub.com

ISBN: 9789357446631

First edition 2022

DEDICATION

I would like to dedicate this to those precious few who have inspired and encouraged me to manifest my creative spirit. Your love will always be softly sheltered in my heart.

"That's Arcadia... when man's soul gets what it deserves... it gets to fly."

- Peter Doherty

ACKNOWLEDGEMENT

Thank you for taking the time to read my words! It truly means more than I could ever express. Gratitude goes especially towards BookLeaf Publishing for this wonderful opportunity. It is unparalleled and I am so blessed to be a part of it.

PREFACE

"Time was the end of riddles,
We were the end of time...

Here were domestic oceans
And a sky that we might reach"

- F. Scott Fitzgerald

"Unless you love someone,
nothing else makes sense."

- E.E Cummings

A Glimpse of Summer

A glimpse of summer in her eyes,
she'll touch and taste an English sky.
In blissful night we run and hide;
and feel the passage of our time.

In wondrous way we walk with ease,
until the sun shakes off the breeze.
By Camden park I doze a while,
as you safeguard a sweet new smile.

Through Venice night we laugh and cry;
and cheer as Scousers sing on high.
We hold the fort through lonesome dark,
until the morning meets the heart.

Between the French dog blues we lay,
forgetting all chaos of day.
A memory to carry through;
as old as one that we both knew.

As two in time we'll take our wine,
and lie here as we are.

A world away, but here I stay:
for you and me tonight.

Library Longing

Wondering why it is so deep,
the secrets that I cannot keep.
She sits a while away, indeed.
To talk to her? Forever's need.

Aflame inside it burns so strong;
in blonde becalm I do belong.
Is she an etch? A fated muse?
Yet still I sit - I cannot choose!

A push I need to spur me on
into the fray of nerve and song.
In future time I'll taste the hand
of God before I leave this land.

Her eyes meet mine and off I go
into the streets of vertigo.
Karima knows, oh yes she does.
But I? Think not, for I'm in love!

Ithaca

He sails away into the sun,
hoping that he will become
a father in those stories told -
before he falls to growing old.

It pains his soul to say goodbye
to all those he's left behind.
I hope one day he will return.
I hope one day he will have learned that

All you really need
is someone to hold, someone who sees
what pain can be.

Off they march into the fight;
once again towards the light.
They long for love, they long for peace;
for gods they know to be appeased.

They laugh, they cry, their sorrows fly.
All the rest, they don't know why.
What will it take for them to see?
What will it take for them to see that

All you really need

is someone to hold, someone who sees
what pain can be.

Years have fallen by as rain,
and washed away all but disdain;
for enemies behind their walls
of stone and greed, how will they fall?

You cast your eyes into the flame;
and hope to see her face again.
The one you know she may not be,
but in her eyes it's clear to see that

All you really need
is someone to hold, someone who sees
what pain can be.

In the end it falls upon
all those who feel they don't belong;
to turn to me and make me see;
to turn to me and make me see that

All I really need
is someone to hold, someone who sees
the pain in me.

A Wise Man Said To Me

Hold onto all your time.
Find someone to love and then
hold on until you die.

He asked me if I needed or
would like another line.
I sheepishly ignored him and fell
back into:

Thank you for the answers.
Thank you for the time.

A kitten is a blessing to
all those who have a knee.
I'll cut you if you tell me that
you're not so heavenly.

Forgive me for intruding,
but for us it's over now.
The world is always waiting
and in truth it's found.

Thank you for the answers.
Thank you for the time in the sun.

A river runs in circles
in the age of irony.
Expect to be forgotten when
you find yourself in need.

Sacrifice your silence
by forgetting how to speak;
and hurry in pursuit of
all that's worthless too.

Thank you for the answers.
Thank you for the time in the sun.

In the sun, in the sun, I'll be waiting in the sun.
In the sun, in the sun, I'll be waiting in the sun,
for you.

Crimson eyes of perfect size,
you touch a part of me
that hasn't seen the light of day since
summer of a dream.

Remember that it's easier to
tell her how you feel.
Don't ever be the shying type;
your love is real.

Thank you for the answers.
Thank you for the time in the sun.

Wake

She looked into the rain,
pondering the ways of the world.
Her father - who caused her so much pain,
but never failed to brighten her day - is gone.

She's grown up now;
but a little girl she'll always be,
sitting on her father's knee.
The stories they made
will never fade; like shadow,
forever caught in shade.

Hope is a difficult thing;
but one should always believe in things one can

never

quite

Summer Only Stays
For A While

Listen to the riverman.
Catch a raindrop in your hand.
She always knew the way to Arcady.

Your pink moon shines as
our daydreams die;
We tried to stay awake for you tonight.

And I want to know where you've been.
And I want to know where you've been.
And I want to go where you've been,
back to summer.

Fall inside, as your reason lies
to a mother, who dances,
alone tonight.

You yearn to cry,
for her heart belies all
the answers to demons that you'll never know.

And I want to know where you've been.

And I want to know where you've been.
And I want to go where you've been,
back to summer.

Walk with me,
as I find my key
to a treasure that's sinking beneath the waves.

Hold her hand,
if it's what you planned.
'cause summer only stays for a while.

My Friend/The Wishing Well

Slipping down the wishing well,
tugging at the straps
of some shoes
that belong to someone else.

Running from what's in my head;
why can't I just go to bed?
My days always end the same.

How we thought the purple street boy
would ever stay the same?
You're fishing for another daydream
in the shallow of your mind.

Just walk on 'round this old town,
and never stop to think of
the love you'll find tonight.

One in three, it's you and me;
to Neverland we fly:
forever entwined in a song.

How we thought the purple street boy
would ever stay the same?
You're fishing for another daydream
in the shallows of your mind.

And I will fly,
before you go home
to the town where you were born.

Please say, please say you love me so.
Please say you love me so.
Please say you love me so.

An English Garden

Sitting all alone in a garden,
we drank away the time -
an old and joyous song.

Wishing all the while that
I would never call you;
but you know I always do.

And I will try to see you home,
through the nights of olden days.

Yes I will.
Yes, I will...

Forever in your eyes, like a fire it will hurt you -
although it's very warm.

"Can you see all the way in time?"
"No."
"Then I'll leave you, 'cause you know I'm very
scared."

And I will try to see you home,
through the nights of olden days.

Through the window of a still car

The lonely boy smokes his only cigarette.

"What's the point?" He grumbles as more cars
pass him by,
taking no notice of the void in which he finds
himself.

*"It isn't fair. Why can't I feel what I want to
feel?"*

A single tear rolls down his cheek, onto
the cigarette.

The boy pauses, then starts to weep.

"Why can't I feel what I want to feel?"

Still the cars take no notice of him.
They never take any notice of him.

And they never will.

April

She smiles into the sadness of his old new brown
eyes.
This view of his soul calls her own heart to fly.
Headlong they burst into the blue night.
"Come on you," she says, *"it'll soon be light!"*

Casanova

Giacomo lacks
not a thing and attracts
all the angels of heaven.

For blemished they're not;
and want they a lot;
so he will offer the key.

From romance to rags
and from rags to riches
they dance together in song.

"You're seriocomic;
all gin but no tonic;
and I know what you want is me!"

Grief

Playing in the puddles of my old street corner;
the most I can see when I go to mourn her.
It's all merely *'seemed'* since last you were here;
when summer she danced, and sunshine was
near.

All The Same

Sat here in the pouring rain,
wishing for another day.
An aching heart is all I feel;
a fantasy that can't be real and

Here we are.
Here we are, all the same.

A bird in Albion I'll be,
to soar in holy harmony.
A shepherd once he was so wise;
but now he's fallen for her eyes and

Here we are.
Here we are, all the same.

Resignedly beneath the sky,
the melancholy waters lie.
For any man who feels the fall,
it's all for one and none for all and

Here we are.
Here we are, all the same.

Oh for a sweet taste of you!

as sunshine on the morning dew.
Away! away! I'll fly to thee;
to find my place in Arcady; and

Here we are.
Here we are, all the same.

Burlesque

Suffering the light of day,
she shuffles on in lonesome way.
A melody is in her ear,
but not the one that you will hear.

Dancing through the door she does
a number for the evening scrubs.
They like her when she twists and turns,
but disregard all of her words.

All as one they sing their song,
until the bell hits half past one.
It's only then she shelves her hair;
and hurries off with evening fare.

Homeward bound she weeps with joy for
every man she did employ.
An empty chaise she does await -
her only friendly face of late.

Waiving on, she whimpers free;
free from all eternity.
If only she could only see;
If only he could only see;
If only we could only see

her.

Fallen Tree

Upon the earth you lie asleep,
as whispers wander secret's keep.
Resting now, your toil is done;
remember days of Pan in song.

Sleep, sleep, sleep and dream
of all that rose before;
of youthful folk who grew beneath
your balming bough forlorn.

In calls to you they seemed to find
a clear 'n' calm, untroubled mind.
But now you dream of time and tide;
and lonely light in morning eye.

A precious pew you do afford
to all who hear the calling chord;
melodic thirds and age old birds
remain a cure for me.

Forget me not, my dear old friend.
I hope one day we'll meet again.

Farewell.

Venus

She wears many masks,
my effervescent lady.
Never faltering in guile,
she'll dance through all my days and all my
nights.

A brush is all she barely needs,
to prove her timeless form.
Painting with her petticoat,
she sings a line so warm.

An ancient muse she used to be;
forgot by some, but remembered by me.
In every face I see her form:
a shelter from the winter storm.

Return with me to my bedly chamber;
and singe my soul with your flame.
I'll kneel and pray beneath your altar,
until my heart is full again.

Lonely, pretty things

In evening time we will be free,
to sail and join her company.

(Awash with stars, the sky she laughs along.)

A lost and lonely empty sea
is one that only we will see.

*"Truth begins in stars above, but ends
in dusty shoes."*

Sail on!

And forget the precious banks of memory;
leave this world in tow.

Letters leave your heart and find themselves
misplaced.
A pity that your heart (as one) can ne'er be
entraced.

*"Will the sun be shine this morn? Or will it just
be long?"*
The eyes of one - a maiden fair - is where I'll
find a song.

A terrible wind is blowing through the corridor
of empty news;
when will we find our home?

By the bottle's end you'll see that I'm shot;
pretending to be such a thing that I'm not.

"Clean up your act!"

Because acting is key.
Time to pretend I'm someone happy.

Again.

Who am "I"?
Who is "he"?
Who are "you"?
And who are "we"?

In evening time we will be free...

George

You're running around a summer garden,
as your mother watches on.
A smile escapes her lips with ease;
and all the worlds belong.

Growing up you dared to dance
through every day and every heart.
Laughter was your remedy:
for every one of them, and me.

I dread to think of all that's lost:
years of time now winter's frost?
No. Your gift to us was more than we;
your gift was positivity!

The key lay in your eyes, I think;
to open all the world.
A timeless soul you'll ever be.
A timeless soul, you're evergreen.

George

Forever End A Day

She shivers in her icy way,
before the day begins.
In open arms she longs to stay,
escaping everything.

Rising up, she takes her tea -
no milk - and sips a while.
amidst lost love she aches to be;
to be beautiful, seen, and free.

Looking at her bed she quakes;
a loneliness in lonely sheets.
A tear that falls is all it takes
to tell her it is time to weep.

"Forever end a day," she sighs,
into the now of mindful eyes.
"Today will not believe itself.
I better run away."

Run away from it all.

Conflict & Resolution?

It's easy to run from the wars,
but peace proves hard to find.
A gun gives sense that all before
is done; and now it is time.

Down in the trenches we ache like tall trees;
forgotten by some, and felled in memory.
It never will end, but fight on! We will cede:
the territory of elites we believe.

So let's raise a glass to long lost young men!
But never forget the hell that holds them.

Her

I can't put my finger on it,
for you will vanish into thin air.
We both lie awake and I'm falling;
in love with you over again.

We're giggling like some small children,
as our film plays on into time.
Our hearts beat out the same rhythm;
with yours is where I feel alive.

The lips that we share are each other's;
and the touch of our flesh is as one.
We'll sink beneath yellow covers;
and hide until we see the sun.

It's always too soon to be over;
It's always too late to begin.
So let's start again, be together;
and live until we see the end.